THE
BLUFFER'S GUIDE
TO
WINE

HARRY EYRES

Published by Oval Books
335 Kennington Road
London SE11 4QE

Telephone: (0171) 582 7123
Fax: (0171) 582 1022
E-mail: info@ovalbooks.com

First published by Ravette Publishing.
This edition published by Oval Books.

First edition1987
Reprinted 1989, 1991
Revised 1992
Reprinted 1993, 1994
New edition 1996
Reprinted 1997, 1998
New edition 1999

Series Editor – Anne Tauté

Cover designer – Jim Wire, Quantum
Printer – Cox & Wyman Ltd

The Bluffer's Guides® series is based
on an original idea by Peter Wolfe.

The Bluffer's Guide®, The Bluffer's
Guides®, Bluffer's®, and Bluff Your
Way® are Registered Trademarks.

CONTENTS

INTRODUCTION

Wine attracts mystique like no other drink and few other subjects. Many people are defeated by wine, thinking that in order to claim any knowledge of it they need:

a) to have visited various vineyards in France
b) to have a cellar (i.e. not a cupboard under the stairs), or
c) to be able to identify exactly where a wine comes from without looking at the label.

This, needless to say, is nonsense. Gone are the days when the wine drinker would ignore anything that didn't come from France, Germany, Spain (only sherry of course) or Portugal (vintage port). Upstarts from the New World like Australia, Chile, South Africa have put themselves firmly on the map; sleeping giants like Italy and Spain are waking up; newcomers like Bulgaria and even Moldova have appeared and surprised everybody with their quality. The message to the bluffer, then, is not to be intimidated by the mystique.

Some knowledge of the old traditions and etiquette is desirable, however, so that you can take on the wine bore at his or her own game and win. It is no longer safe, alas, to follow the inspired advice to confine yourself to completely meaningless remarks like "Too many tramlines".

This guide sets out to conduct you through the main danger zones: places and circumstances in which you are most likely to encounter wine and the wine expert, and to equip you with a vocabulary and an evasive technique that will minimise the risk of your being found out.

THE BASICS

What is Wine?

There is no argument about this, wine is fermented grape juice. People may make, drink and even talk about elderflower wine, peach wine, kiwi-fruit wine or whatever, but you do not need to know about them. On no account discuss them. They have no mystique and thus no bluffing potential. Non-alcoholic wines are not wines. Wines, like some human beings, have an absolute need to be alcoholic.

The Three Colours

Wine comes in three basic colours:

Red – which ranges from purple to light brown

White – which is usually pale yellow

Rosé – which is to be avoided (unless it comes from Navarra).

It is also capable of being green (vinho verde), black (Cahors), and blush (a fine example of unparalleled marketing lunacy).

Sweet and Dry

First it is as well to remember that anything calling itself medium is in fact **sweet**. Second, all wines (except those made from grapes affected by the noble rot) are naturally **dry**. The sweetness comes either from stopping the fermentation before all the sugar has been converted to alcohol, or from adding unfermented grape-juice, or from adding sugar, usually in liquid form.

All this does not mean that you should scorn sweet wines. The ignorant have turned their noses up at them for so long that a very rewarding bluffing line can be cultivated in, say, the little-known sweet white wines of the Loire, or the really fine German Auslesen, Beerenauslesen, and Trockenbeerenauslesen. It is a relief to know that the last two can be shortened to BA and TBA. If you want to create a frisson, recommend an Austrian TBA from a place called Rust.

Fortification

Most wines are unfortified, that is to say they have only the alcohol provided by God in the form of sun and grapes (plus sugar beet in the 'must' if they are French). But some wines, like port, sherry, madeira and the two venerable old white wines, marsala and malaga, are strengthened by the addition of anything from brandy to industrial alcohol. Fortified wines, like fortified towns, are not to be taken lightly. They get you buzzing more quickly but land you with the most appalling after-effects if you're not careful.

Still or Sparkling

This should be self-explanatory. Wines come in either thick heavy bottles with corks wrapped round with wire which are impossible to get out, in which case they are **sparkling** (i.e. fizzy, but for some reason this word must not be used of wines), or in ordinary bottles with ordinary corks, which are impossible to get out, in which case they are **still**.

The fun begins when you discover that many still wines are slightly fizzy, or rather, sparkling. Sometimes this is intentional, as with vinho verde. Even when it is not intentional, it is not necessarily considered a fault. The thing to do, in any case, is to say "Hmm... slightly pétillant" (if it's French) or "Possibly spritzig" (if it's German).

Essential Equipment

Unless you can pass yourself off as a wine writer, cash is indispensable. Unlike some other art-forms, wine has to be bought and consumed to be appreciated. There are, however, a few other essentials:

1. A Nose

Ninety per cent of the taste of a wine is perceived via the nose. You will appreciate this if you have a bad cold. The most famous nose in the wine business is possessed by Don José Ignacio Domecq of the well known sherry firm: this is long and beaky and fits conveniently inside the small, tapered sherry glasses called copitas. It is probably a case of natural selection. Non-sherry tasters do not need such an impressive proboscis, but the equipment inside it must be operative.

2. A Corkscrew

Decent wine comes in bottles with corks for which, unfortunately, no really satisfactory device for extraction has yet been invented. One can understand why, in the old days, choleric gentlemen used to decapitate bottles with red-hot pincers, but this is sadly out of fashion, and in any case difficult without a blazing fire. You should probably opt for the 'waiter's friend' or the screwpull, particularly the lever model screwpull which at the price of a plane ticket from London to Bordeaux is only for the serious, but enables even little old ladies to extract the most stubborn cork without perspiring.

Types of corkscrew to be avoided include the bulbous Russian doll variety (you can't see what you're doing with it and the handle tends to come off mid-screw), the double-armed ratchet type (which has a drill-like action that can bore a hole through the cork, and it catches your fingers in its ratchets), or the vacuum variety which pumps the air out. This can blow up the bottle.

Go for the simplest kind so long as it has a good wire worm screw and a comfortable, firmly attached handle. This has good inverted bluffing potential and the great advantage of working.

3. A Glass

It is generally agreed that wine should be drunk from a glass, though for the desperate, any water-tight receptacle will do. Glasses have the advantage of not affecting the flavour as leather bottles, metal goblets and dancing slippers do. You can also see what you're drinking.

The kind of glass is relatively unimportant, though a tulip shape, which gathers the **bouquet** (see Smell) is considered best for most wines. Otherwise, the simpler the better: it's easier to wash up.

4. A Decanter

Simply removing the cork to allow a wine to breathe is useless because the surface area exposed to the air is so small. The only way to let it breathe properly is to pour some into a glass when you open the bottle. This not only increases the breathing area but enables you to justify sneaking a glass ahead of the game.

A decanter is not strictly necessary, except for old red wines and vintage and crusted ports which have muck in the bottom of the bottle. No-one can decide whether or not one should decant burgundy. Decanting, apart from separating the wine from the muck, exposes it to the atmosphere and therefore lets it breathe. Some wines, however, especially very old ones, do not take well to the atmosphere and fade away. Decanting very old wines, therefore, is a risky business.

White wines, including sherry, should not be decanted. It is unnecessary, and indeed harmful to the wine, and besides, the visual effect could be unpleasantly medical (which is perhaps why white wine is usually put in green bottles). On the other hand, by all means decant an inexpensive port if you want to pass it off as vintage.

Decanting is the process of pouring the contents into a decanter and stopping before the muck gets in. It sounds easy. It is easy. But it must be made to look as difficult as possible. The aim is to make the performance resemble a Black Mass. A candle must be used, supposedly to show when the sediment reaches the neck, but in fact to induce ceremonial atmosphere. Absolute silence must be observed and a look of rapt concentration maintained, until the last drop of clear liquid has been transferred.

After this, a dramatic sigh, wipe of the brow and momentary indication of emotional exhaustion, as of an actor having just played a great tragic role, may be called for to underline the risk involved. It is particularly important to sniff the cork of the bottle being decanted: it may then be attached to the neck of the decanter. This is roughly equivalent to the handing back to the patient of an organ which has been surgically removed.

Cellar and Storage

Bluffers should not be afraid to talk about their cellar even if they do not possess anything remotely approximating an underground storeroom. A cellar for these purposes is a collection of at least two bottles, or possibly a single bottle, of reasonable quality. If you are keeping wine for any length of time, however, there are two important rules to observe.

1. To avoid the corks drying out and letting air in, bottles should be kept lying down (on their side)* or better still, upside down. This will look impressively eccentric, but is in fact the normal way for bottles to lie when being transported or stored.

2. Wine should be kept somewhere with a reasonably constant temperature, preferably not above 60°F 15.5°C (a fairly cool day). This is likely to be impossible to achieve, in which case remember a constant

*But be sure to point out that latest research shows that, uniquely, champagne should be stored upright rather than horizontal.

11

temperature of 70°F (21°C) is better than a fluctuation between 40°F (4.5°C) and 60°F (15.5°C). Or simply drink your wine quickly before it has a chance to go off.

Poor cellaring conditions have one advantage, namely that wine will mature more quickly in them. Certain Bordeaux vintages which have taken ages to come round (1970, 1975) might be greatly improved by a spell in a centrally heated flat.

Serving Temperature

The concern about serving wine at the right temperature can lead people to extreme measures like baking claret in the oven or icing Sauternes. These are probably inadvisable, though wine is surprisingly resilient. The rule is that most red wines should be served at room temperature (the French term is 'chambré') and most white wines lightly chilled, that is to say, having spent an hour in the fridge or twelve minutes in the freezer. Wine snobs tend to be suspicious of the freezer which suggests that they once forgot to take wine out of it.

There is an intermediate state between chilled and chambré, namely cellar temperature. This is a very useful category, because it can mean the temperature the wine happens to be when you have forgotten to chill or warm it. Some light red wines like Beaujolais are best quaffed at this temperature anyway.

If a red wine is too cold, you can suggest your guests warm it by cupping the glass in their hands. Use the French 'chaleur de la main' to add further refinement.

History

The history of wine is very long and involved, stretching back as it does to way before Roman times. Mercifully you need deal only with the last one hundred years because the vines in Europe, Africa, and very nearly everywhere else, were all but wiped out by a plague of aphids. This affliction, phylloxera vastatrix, attacked and destroyed the roots of the vines. Fortunately for us it took nearly 30 years to do so. During that time wine growers had a chance to import native vine stocks from the United States, and graft what remained of the famous grape varieties on to them.

Now, ironically, phylloxera is destroying Californian vineyards, the Californians having planted European vines on less than totally phylloxera-resistant roots.

It may still be possible to find a doddering ancient who can remember the last bottle of pre-phylloxera wine. But unless you are a grey-bearded loon of phenomenal age there is no point in your trying this.

TASTING AND DRINKING

Bluffers should never forget that tasting and drinking are two distinct activities and should not be confused.

Tasting is an unpleasant professional activity which people do to earn a living. It is done standing up, and involves rude noises, wry faces and spittoons.

Tasters *never* swallow. Well, hardly ever. One man in a pinstripe suit at a smart London tasting was heard asking another, 'What do you think of the Niederhäuser Hermannshöhle Spätlese 1985?' The other man paused judiciously before replying, 'I honestly don't know, but it slips down a treat.'

Drinking, on the other hand, is pleasure. It is done sitting down, except at drinks parties, which are in any case seldom a pleasure. It is true that if you are drinking decent wine, you should go through some of the motions of tasting, but you will do so in a different spirit.

The motions of tasting are the following:

1. Pour out a little wine, filling the glass no more than a quarter full. Stare fixedly at it. Look mean. If it is red, tilt the glass and hold it against a white surface. Viewing the **meniscus** (where the surface of the liquid meets the glass) against a white background shows the wine's true colour very clearly. It also provides a perfect excuse to hold your glass against other more interesting white surfaces such as a white blouse or shirt front. (It is a fact that only one wine shows a greenish tinge at the meniscus, *viz* sherry. But it is probably easier to rely on the fact that it says 'Sherry' on the bottle.)

2. Hold the glass firmly by the base and twirl it round either clockwise or anti-clockwise, but not both at the same time. Twirling does require a little practice: too vigorous a twirl will send the wine sloshing over the edge, too little vigour will have no effect on the wine whatsoever. The theory is that it releases the bouquet. In fact, it proves that you are a pro.

3. Having twirled, sniff. Here an impressively shaped nose undoubtedly helps. Blocked sinuses do not. Some people favour moving the nose from side to side over the wine, presumably to give each nostril its share, but this can look rather sinister.

4. Only after these preliminaries is it permissible to take liquid into your mouth. A fairly large sip, in contrast to the small measure in the glass, is the thing, but not too large to enable you to perform the most difficult trick, which is to take in a small amount of air with an audible sucking noise at the same time as the wine. This is supposed to aerate the wine in your mouth and release more flavour. It is not the same as gargling. Try to avoid gargling – unless you have a sore throat. Wine, after all, is an antiseptic.

5. Having swilled it about a bit, spit the wine out as elegantly as possible into a spittoon, box of sawdust or potted plant. There is a marked spitting order at some tastings. Watch out for this or you will get indelible young claret upon your front. Mind you, it is very easy to put it there yourself.

6. Surreptitiously drink some of the wine you liked best.

7. Take notes on all stages except (6).

When drinking a good wine, or one that your host considers good, limit yourself to tilting, twirling and sniffing. Do these things in a gracious, smiling manner, rather than with the fixed, suspicious glare of the professional taster. Do not try to take in air with the wine. You may not be asked again.

A drinker should not fill his glass more than half full if he is going to attempt twirling. He may feel that this is too great a sacrifice.

Talking about Wine

For some reason, many people feel that drinking, or even tasting and drinking, wine is not enough: they must also talk about it. Indeed social gatherings among the wine-loving fraternity seem to revolve almost solely around talk about wine. You may secretly find this boring or pretentious, but clearly as a bluffer you need not only to be able to drink and taste wine properly but also to hold up your end in wine-speak.

This is a complicated subject, but a few simple rules can get you a surprisingly long way.

1. Do not use words except where strictly necessary. Noises either non-committal ("Hmmm....") or enthusiastic ("Mmm.... Aah!") and facial contortions (raised eyebrows, narrowed glance, pursed lips) are often adequate, and do not commit you to anything.

2. The word "Yes" is quite sufficient in most cases. It

can be said in an infinite variety of tones – doubtful, quizzical, interrogative, tentative, affirmative, decisive, appreciative, ecstatic. It can be repeated, in a clipped, conversation-stopping manner ("Yes. Yes."), or in a rising, excited tone ("Yesyesyes!").

3. Put off describing what the wine actually tastes like for as long as possible. Limit yourself to some of the following technical expressions as far as you can.

   a) Mention **ullage**. This means the level of wine in the bottle. If you have noticed that the bottle is not completely full, say in a neutral tone "Ah, slightly ullaged". It could be, of course, that your host has swigged some of it beforehand.

   b) Ask whether the wine has "thrown a **deposit**". Deposit, of course, refers to the muck in the bottom of the bottle, not to what you get back when you return the empties to the off-licence.

   c) If it is a red wine, and you have noticed when tilting it that it leaves a thick transparent trail on the glass (most red wines do), say that it has "good legs".

Appearance

When you have exhausted these gambits, talk about the colour. You are on fairly safe ground here unless you are colour-blind, since it is easier to describe visual phenomena than tastes or smells. It might be a good idea to mug up your metals and semi-precious stones: different shades of gold, amber, garnet, ruby etc. seem to go down particularly well.

Smell

When talking about smell, do not use the word 'smell'. In English this usually has unpleasant connotations. Choose instead from **nose** (which with wine does not have unpleasant associations), **aroma** or **bouquet**, if you're feeling flowery.

If the wine doesn't smell of anything, and you know you do not have a cold, try "Rather dumb on the nose, don't you find?" or "Still very closed-up".

Alternatively, if it smells very strongly, you can say, "It's very forward on the nose". None of these comments, of course, commits you to an opinion of the wine's quality.

If you have to become more specific, here are some of the more commonly used 'nose' words:

oaky, buttery, vanilla-ey – all used, interchangeably it seems, to describe certain wines which spend a considerable time in oak barrels, especially red Rioja and white Burgundy and its Californian and Australian clones.

blackcurranty – only use when you have checked that the wine is made from the Cabernet Sauvignon grape.

spicy – only used when you know that the wine is made from the Gewürztraminer grape. This is a very vague term considering how many different spices there are, but such things do not worry the cognoscenti.

Of course, people will say wines smell of anything; violets, truffles (both the kind pigs dig up in Perigord and the delicious, dusted chocolate balls), beetroots, sweaty saddles, wet socks, farmyards, petrol (used of old Rieslings, which can have a curious oily whiff, and best said, like so many things, in French – "goût de pétrole"). The noble pinot noir, from which red burgundy is fashioned, is particularly prone to the odour of ordure. A wine-writer said of a burgundy, with the air of one bestowing a compliment, 'Bags of pooh!'.

Smells are oddly evocative, but often these correspondences seem entirely personal and do not work for others. There is nothing to stop you trying this kind of thing, the more personal the better, because it cannot then be disproved. For instance, "This wine reminds me of one evening I spent in Crete. I don't know exactly what the connection is – the wild thyme, the sea-air, the flock of goats in the distance..."

Describing Wine

It is a truth universally acknowledged that there are few words to describe tastes – sweet, dry, acid are simply not enough. There isn't even a generally agreed word for the opposite of acid, and it is doubtful whether there are other definitive words to describe the taste of wine, since few wines are either salty or bitter enough for those two other unmistakable qualities to come into play. All the rest is metaphor – a poet's dream, but a bluffer's nightmare. Before you despair, quite a lot of mileage can be got out of the three main words.

Sweetness and Dryness

Degrees of **sweetness** and **dryness** are perhaps on the obvious side, but in wine-speak there is no harm in stating the obvious. It is particularly useful if you know how sweet or how dry a wine is meant to be, and then can suggest that it somehow contradicts expectations. Thus, "Surprisingly dry for a Sauternes/ Beerenauslese" or "This Chablis isn't as bone dry as I would have expected" are effective because they show others that:

a) you know your stuff
b) you have original, even if wrong, opinions.

Almost all red wines, incidentally, are dry. There is not much point in saying that a claret (bordeaux) is dry; if you try to be original and opine that your host's Château Lafite is surprisingly sweet, you may not be given a second glass.

Acidity

You can get further by talking about **acidity**. Acidity in wine, funnily enough, is generally considered a good thing, and so the comment 'Good acidity' can work wonders. This is especially true of white wines, in which acidity is synonymous with freshness. A white wine with too little acidity can be criticised for being heavy, flat or simply fat (see Body).

Wines can, of course, be too acid. This tends to be a fault of wines from cold countries and regions like Germany, Champagne and England. Comments on excess acidity are often expressed in involuntary, physical forms.

Wine, without getting too technical, contains different kinds of acidity. The best kinds, tartaric and lactic for instance, do not have a pronounced taste but impart freshness (or zinginess) to the wine. There are other kinds of acidity which do have a marked taste: malic acid makes wine taste like apples, not necessarily a bad thing. 'Appley' is a good word to use of Mosel wines, for instance. The worst kind of acidity is acetic, also known as vinegar. If you think a wine tastes vinegary, but don't want to upset your host, say, "This wine has rather high volatile acidity, don't you think?" It isn't considered nearly so rude.

Balance

Even good acidity on its own is not enough: a wine needs to be balanced. **Balance** is perhaps the key concept in the wine world. Fortunately nobody ever asks exactly what is balanced with what: the idea is that all the constituent parts of a wine, alcohol, acidity, fruit, are roughly in harmony.

Unlike unbalanced people, unbalanced wines do not do unpredictable things: in fact they are usually very ordinary. A perfectly balanced wine is a rare and wonderful thing.

Tannin

Here is a more friendly term for the bluffer. **Tannin** is a preservative substance extracted from the grape skins, pips and stems, mainly found in red wines. It is easily recognisable because it grips the back of your teeth, rather like those little sucker things the dentist puts in your mouth. Like the dentist, tannin leaves your teeth in need of the services of a hygienist. Young red wines which are the opposite of mellow are likely to be tannic.

Hard and **tannic** are two adjectives which commonly go together, particularly when you are tasting young claret, one of the most unpleasant of all aesthetic experiences. If you are given a claret and find it about as attractive and yielding as a Scottish bank manager, you may say "Still rather tannic, I find." There is a danger here: some wines (especially clarets) like some bank managers, no doubt, pass from being unpleasantly hard and tannic (i.e. too young) to being unpleasantly 'dried out' (i.e. too old) without any intervening stage of pleasant mellowness.

Fruit

This might seem the most obvious quality of a wine's taste. But **fruit** is the starting-point of wine, the substance it is made from. Thus to say that a wine is fruity is to suggest that it has gone through all the processes which have transformed it from uninteresting grapes into a miraculous drink, for nothing.

'Fruity' should be the bluffer's last resort. 'Grapey' is a somewhat different matter, because only wines made from certain kinds of grape, especially Muscat, actually taste, or should taste of grapes.

Body

This is an essential description. Unlike women, wines generally aspire to be **full-bodied**. Wines with insufficient body are said to be 'thin', which is not a compliment. On the other hand, wines with too much body can be called 'fat', which is slightly insulting. Male wine people, particularly after a glass or two, are prone to talk of wine in female terms (especially the Germans) thus: "This is the beautiful girl you take to the Opera ...and this is the woman you marry."

There are, of course, all kinds of other approaches to talking about the taste of wine. There is some famous advice to be 'boldly meaningless' and talk about 'cornery wines' and other such things. You can always try long German words. Then there is the *Brideshead Revisited* style, abominably precious ('Shy, like a gazelle') but possibly due for resuscitation.

At the other extreme there is the blunt Antipodean approach prevalent down under, such as 'Not a wine to wrap around your tonsils.'

Finally, there is one all-embracing term you can offer, and that is **pronounced**. "This wine has a pronounced bouquet, don't you think?" is a comment which is both safe and more or less meaningless which is what the bluffer is aiming at, after all.

Great Vintages of the Past

Vintages are like 18th-century battles. The French win most of them, the Germans put in the occasional brilliant victory, and the Italians don't try.

It could be impressive, though probably completely useless, to be able to reel off a few of the great years of the past:

* The year of Halley's comet, 1811, and the year of Revolutions, 1848, are two quite easy ones to remember (probably easier to remember than to drink).

- Then 1870 (the clarets of that year took 80 years to come round, which must have been mortifying for the original purchasers), and the great pair of 1899 and 1900.

- Good vintages quite often come in pairs: 1928 and 1929, 1961 and 1962, 1970 and 1971, and 1982 and 1983, 1985 and 1986, 1994 and 1995.

- On the other hand, good vintages also come singly: 1945, 1959, 1966. Or in trios: 1947, 1948, 1949; 1988, 1989, 1990.

There are several things to note here:

a) that when talking about great vintages people always seem to mean great *claret* vintages.

b) that great claret vintages now come on average about two years out of three.

c) that vintages of the century occur at least twice a decade.

If someone says, 'Of course, 1928 was a wonderful vintage for claret,' you can try retorting, "Yes, but very poor for Tokay" or "Yes, but a freak rainstorm practically destroyed the vintage in the Barossa valley." It is highly unlikely the other person will know anything about old vintages in obscure areas.

BUYING WINE

Impulse buying of wine, as with cars, is invariably fatal. Prepare for buying by deciding whether you want wine for drinking with an appreciative friend, a dinner party, for immediate consumption or for laying down. Next, decide what price per bottle you can afford for your purposes and stick to it.

You have four options as to where to buy:

Supermarkets

These have obvious advantages: you can buy lettuce and Château Lafite (well, almost) at one and the same time. Because they are so big they can sell more cheaply – but they are also very good at convincing you they are less expensive than anywhere else when this is not necessarily the case. More to the point, they have good ranges of wine. But they also have a serious disadvantage: if you do find a nice wine in a supermarket and serve it to your friends, there is every chance they will know exactly where it comes from and exactly how much it costs. "This Château Bon Marché of yours is very nice. Much nicer than the one I bought last week."

Wine Warehouses

These sprang into prominence because they had a 'real', functional appeal, like places to eat called kitchens or granaries – the idea being that you are cutting out the smooth middleman and getting the product, with a few rough edges, at source. In fact warehouses are not warehouses at all, just retail outlets like anywhere else. On other hand, some do sell excellent wines very cheaply. They also do the very sensible thing of allowing you to taste wines before buying. With very inexpensive wines you will say that this is not merely an advantage, it is a necessity.

Off-licences and High Street Chains

These used to come bottom of the list. They are still the source of most of the dreaded double-litres of Valpolicella which give unpleasant post-prandial effects. Their prices are often scandalous and it is unusual to see bottles properly stored in them. The people who run them tend to own savage Alsatian dogs to guard the till. However, chains have one advantage: they are open at the times you need them most.

Specialist Wine Merchants and Shops

These are likely to be smaller and friendlier. They may even have people in them who know something about wine.

Wine at Auction

A lot of wine finds its way to the auction rooms as a last resort, or, quite simply, because it has gone off. There are bargains to be had as well, but it is a high-risk area and you are earnestly advised to taste before buying. Some auction houses hold regular pre-sale tastings. If you wish for a free glass there is no point in arriving more than half an hour after the starting time – they tend to fill up with free-loaders. Disgraceful really; some people will do anything for a glass or two.

Understanding the Label

There is one further obstacle in the path of appreciating wine, that of deciphering the sometimes arcane and confusing information printed on the label. The worst offenders here are undoubtedly the Germans, who compound the sin of overcomplicating their wine nomenclature with the use of unreadable Gothic types. If you can understand a German wine label, you can understand anything.

French wine labels, on the other hand, are the leaders in sheer pretentiousness:

Grand Vin de Bordeaux – Well, Bordeaux's a big area: the wine may not be all that grand.

Château la Tour de Saint Hippolyte – Some jumped-up little wine is trying to bask in reflected glory.

Appellation Bordeaux Supérieur Contrôlée – Don't get too excited, the superior just means it has a degree more alcohol.

Cuvée fûts neufs – Oh no, it tastes like a DIY cabinet.

Millésime 1995 – Don't take this too seriously, it's just a printed number.

Mis en Bouteille au Domaine – Some guy with a mobile bottling line comes round to the back yard.

French Wine made by Australians – The Aussies are getting their own back.

If German wine labels contain too much information (and they do), others contain too little. Greek wines are particular offenders: not only named after Greek gods (Aphrodite, Bacchus), tragic heroes (Othello, Orestes) or, mystifyingly, lavatory cleansers (Demestica), their labels tell you nothing about the vintage, region or anything else you want to know. On the other hand, given the quality of most Greek wines, this may be a sensible policy.

In general, things to look out for on labels so as to hold forth in the appropriate direction, are:

The vintage – This is usually clearly visible. Some wines are non-vintage, but you know that the only acceptable non-vintage wines are sherry (which hardly ever has a vintage), and champagne.

The grape variety – Don't expect this in all cases. The aristocratic wines (claret and burgundy, for instance) do not specify their grape variety: you are expected to know it.

The country of origin – Always look out for this: some bottles carry the mark of shame 'EC Tafelwein'. This means they have been dredged up from the Community Wine Lake and bottled by bureaucrats.

The region – Look out for initials like A.C., D.O.C., which tell you the wine comes from a designated area. With Italian wines this is mostly a bad thing.

Bottling information – Whether the wine has been bottled at the Château (always considered a good thing), or estate, in the country of origin, or in England (always considered a bad thing).

Grape Varieties

There are more than 4,000 named varieties of the domesticated vine. Don't panic. It would be a bold person who claimed to be able to distinguish more than 30 by taste, and for practical purposes you will be able to get by with less than a dozen.

1. Cabernet Sauvignon

The most famous red Bordeaux grape, now also grown in California, Australia, Spain, Italy, Bulgaria, Chile, Moldova, etc. It has in fact become the world's No. 1 grape. This could be because wines made from it taste rather like Ribena. They also taste roughly the same wherever the grape is grown, which is useful as you know what you'll get.

2. Chardonnay

The grape used to make white burgundy, and (with two red ones) champagne. It, too, is grown successfully in California, Australia, Spain, Italy, Bulgaria, Chile, etc. The world's No. 1 white grape, it also tends to taste roughly the same wherever it is grown.

3. Chenin Blanc

A white grape grown in the Loire valley and also in South Africa. Probably the most revolting grape variety in the world, it generally produces wines which smell and taste of vomit. In favoured corners of the Loire it does somehow manage to come up with some of the best dry and sweet wines in the world. In less favoured corners, it produces a lot of ordinary sparkling wine.

4. Gewürztraminer

(Also known as Traminer, but that was apparently too short and easy to pronounce.) This grape, mainly grown in Alsace, imparts a very pronounced, supposedly spicy aroma and rich flavour. You either love it or hate it.

5. Merlot

The other red Bordeaux grape, also grown in California, Italy, Bulgaria, Chile, etc. It often makes more palatable wines than Cabernet Sauvignon, less tough and tannic, but it is deemed to be not as good, possibly because wines made from it *don't* taste of Ribena.

6. Pinot Noir

Red grape of notoriously difficult, temperamental character. An artistic type which, like Solzhenitsyn, Ovid and Oscar Wilde, goes into a decline when exiled, in this case from its native lands of Burgundy and Champagne.

7. Riesling

The most important thing is to pronounce it properly, 'Reezling' not 'Ryezling'. The next most important thing is to be aware that a lot of so-called Riesling, e.g. Welsch Riesling, grown confusingly in Slovakia, and the Lutomer Riesling, is not real Riesling at all. The true Riesling is the best German grape and makes rather tart wines which you may correctly call 'steely'. When they get older, you call them 'petrolly', after the little known variant called Diesling which is used to fuel taxis.

8. **Sauvignon Blanc**

Fashionable white grape variety, it is pretty tart and supposed to impart the smell of crushed nettles. This is the grape that is used to make Sancerre and Pouilly Fumé, which is why in California (where they grow it, like everything else) it is called Fumé Blanc.

9. **Sémillon**

Possibly the world's most undervalued white grape The noble rot (see Glossary) likes to attack it, especially in Sauternes. The Australians are going for it in a big way as well, and it seems to thrive on it.

10. **Syrah**

Possibly the world's most undervalued red grape, used to make the great northern Rhône wines. The Aussies like this one as well, but call it Shiraz.

Other grape varieties to look out for are:

Gamay – A purple grape used to make Beaujolais, but, perhaps not surprisingly, not much else.

Muscadet – A grape variety which gives its name to a wine and doesn't taste of anything much, not to be confused with.

Muscat – A grape which *does* impart a very strong taste (of Muscat).

For really obscure varieties, try the French Viognier (only used to make Condrieu and Château Grillet), the Catalan Xarel-lo with its unique hyphenated double 'l', and the German Ortega (also grown in England) named after the Spanish philosopher Ortega y Gasset. Nobody knows why.

WINE AROUND THE WORLD

The Cult of the Winemaker

The cult started in California. 'Soil is dirt,' proclaimed Bill Jekel of Monterey County (an understandable sentiment if you live in Monterey), 'the winemaker is king'. It was the Promethean myth of the winemaker as hero able to take a neutral raw material and transform nature into whatever he or she (though usually he) chose.

Many supermarkets have fallen for this, and state the name of the winemaker on the back label of some very ordinary wine. The general rule is that these names are not real winemakers at all but glossy front-people for large wine-making organisations which employ young trainees at the dirty end. But the wheel is now turning and even in California winemakers have taken to saying that, surprisingly enough, quality is determined mainly by the grapes from which the wine is made.

Flying winemakers became all the rage in the early 1990s. Clean-cut, young, mainly Anglo-Saxon men in suits seemed to be engaged in a competition to see who could clock up most air miles as they jetted around overseeing harvests in Chile, South Africa Australia, Hungary, even France. The names to drop are Hugh Ryman (who, the rumour goes, has now been propagated by clonal selection into an unspecified number of identical Hugh Rymans), Jacques Lurton (a more unpredictable Frenchman of flair) and Kym Milne, who lives in London and does his flying wine-making by remote control. All you need say of all this activity is that is has produced "A mass of inexpensive, inoffensive wines lacking regional character".

France

French wine has taken so much of a slating in recent years that some bluffing points could be scored by making a modest defence of the old wine country's virtues of civilised elegance, restraint and finesse. However, most French wines have been seriously overrated for decades. Many are still made from unripe grapes beefed up by the addition of sugar during fermentation (chaptalisation). A great number still trade on ancient names which routinely fail to deliver value for money.

Languedoc-Roussillon

A bold but reliable line is to poo-poo most classic French areas (Bordeaux, Burgundy, Chablis, Muscadet, etc.) and heap praise upon the formerly despised 'backyard' of Languedoc-Roussillon. If your companion expresses disbelief and suggests 'Isn't that the source of most of the wine in the EU wine lake?' you are well set up. Fix your interlocutor with a withering glare and retort: "The region has undergone a complete metamorphosis in the last ten years." Go on to mention Robert Skalli (the wizard of Sète, and inventor of varietal vins de pays) and the influx of Australian producers and winemakers – some of whom cheekily label their product 'French wine made by Australians'.

The Terroir Argument

A reasonably well clued-up wine bore might mutter something at this point about the dreary sameness of wine made from international grape varieties. Here you produce your trump card – Aimé Guibert of Mas de Daumas Gassac (the 's' of Mas is voiced), self-appointed defender of the entire French peasant (or paysan) tradition. The future of Languedoc-Roussillon lies with the terroiristes you should insist, perhaps banging the table for emphasis. If others express doubt about the dubious quality of some supermarket Fitou, Corbières or Minervois (Languedoc appellations), ask whether the grapes were grown on "schistous" soil. That should silence them.

Though Languedoc-Roussillon is the up-and-coming French region, some skeletal knowledge of the more classic wines and areas is probably advisable to guard against the persistent wine snob.

Bordeaux

The line to take with Bordeaux is that it no longer has much to do with wine, much more to do with investment, insurance and finance. Many of the top Bordeaux châteaux are now owned by insurance or finance companies (Latour, Pichon-Longueville, Beychevelle, Gruaud-Larose) whose directors are presumably about the only people able to afford to drink their produce.

In the meantime, there are a few facts you should know. Bordeaux is one of the Englishman's wines and as such is known (for no good reason) as **claret**. The English owned Bordeaux for much of the Middle Ages and the great château wines were developed for the British in the 17th century. Thus, the French are notoriously ignorant about claret.

Bordeaux (claret) is the most aristocratic of all wines. In 1855 the Bordeaux châteaux were divided into a system of 1st, 2nd, 3rd, 4th and 5th classed growths. Few are malignant, but you should argue that the classification is absurdly outdated. Say that the bourgeois growths such as Chasse-Spleen, Poujeaux and Pibran are infinitely better than many classed growths. Produce a little-known château from one of the Bordeaux satellite areas such as Bourg, Blaye or Côtes de Castillon and say it is just as good as many famous names. (Note the 'many', which does not commit you to dismissing them all.) It may not be, but it will certainly be one you can afford.

After a string of successes in the 1980s Bordeaux became arrogant and assumed it could expect a good vintage every year. Nature retaliated with some dreadful rainy vintages in 1991, 1992, 1993 and 1994. The Bordelais claimed they were able to reverse the effects of torrential rain during the vintage with new techniques such as inverse osmosis, cold concentration under vacuum and heavy hype.

Burgundy

Two approaches are possible here. The first is an even more contemptuous chuckle than that with which you greeted Bordeaux: "The Burgundians are living in the Middle Ages. The weather is atrocious, the wine-making techniques – which include naked men plunging into the fermenting vats to get things started – often faulty, the subdivision of properties a joke, the prices a scandal. Few people are gullible enough to shell out huge sums for mediocre Burgundy." Not only, as wine expert Anthony Hanson said, does Burgundy smell of shit, most of it is over-priced.

The second approach is more indulgent. "Burgundy is impossibly complicated, and the wines poor value. But it can be *so* rewarding. When you track down that obscure, perfect bottle, the pleasure is incomparable."

Take your pick, but if you choose the latter you will need to know some of the smart names. The line with Burgundy is that the grower is all-important – and the vintage often unfairly associated with the same vintage in Bordeaux. Dismiss the big-merchant houses (négociants) with the exception of Jadot, Joseph Drouhin, Louis Latour (for whites; scorn the famously pasteurised reds). Name the smart new small négociants, Olivier Leflaive (of the same family as the famous but inconsistent Domaine Leflaive) and Verget. The most famous estate in Burgundy is the Domaine de la Romanée-Conti. It has monopoly of some of Burgundy's greatest vineyards (Romanée-Conti, La Tache) but one's real awe and amazement should be reserved for the stratospheric prices the estate charges – and the perfectly straight face the director Aubert de Villaine manages to keep while charging them.

De Villaine had a dramatic falling out with co-owner Lalou Bize-Leroy who went off in a huff and concentrated on her other wines made at Domaine Leroy by biodynamic methods, which involve preparations of dung and gazing at the moon.

The Loire

Of the Loire there is a good argument for sticking to the châteaux and forgetting the wines, which are noted mainly for their unrelentingly high acidity. They also tend to be made from the repellent Chenin Blanc grape. Two exceptions are Muscadet and Sancerre. One of the best-kept secrets in wine is that Muscadet does not taste of anything to speak of (it is extremely hard to identify in blind tastings). Sancerre and its neighbour, Pouilly-Fumé, on the other hand, are the easiest to identify by taste (nettles, old brie).

It is a good idea to overlook these popular names. They are, in any case, not the best Loire wines, which you know to be the dry Savonnières, medium Vouvray, and the sweet Bonnezeaux (pronounced 'bonzo') and Quarts de Chaume ('cardeshowm'). The last two are much better than the well-publicised Moulin Touchais and very few people have heard of them. They are absurdly good value as a result.

There is also some good bluffing potential to be had from the red wines of the Loire. The best of these is Bourgeuil, which is made from the Cabernet Franc grape and is about as close to Ribena as you can get without infringing the patent.

The vintage should usually be the latest or the one before that. Conversely, with the sweet wines, the older the better.

The Rhône

Ignored for much of modern history because they were out of reach of both the English and the French court, the wines of the Rhône are now highly modish. The first thing to remember about the Rhône is that it is divided into north and south. Northern Rhône is expensive, exclusive and divided into small villages. Southern Rhône is less expensive less exclusive and divided into larger villages (e.g. Châteauneuf-du-Pape). The second thing to remember about the Rhône is that the reds are much better than the whites, which can mostly be forgotten. However important exceptions are the wines made from the ultra-trendy Viognier grape, Condrieu, Château-Grillet and one or two mavericks from the south such as Domaines Sainte Anne and Pélaquié.

The first northern Rhône wine to mention is Côte-

Rôtie. Rhapsodise about Guigal's absurdly expensive single-vineyard bottlings, La Mouline, La Landonne and La Turque. No-one can actually afford to buy these wines so you can say more or less anything about them without fear of challenge. Move on to Hermitage, the most historic of northern Rhône reds: here Gérard Chave is king of the small growers. Among négociants, say that Chapoutier (now toying with biodynamic methods) is improving faster than former leader Jaboulet. Cornas used to be considered a more rustic appellation but is now just as expensive as Côte-Rôtie and Hermitage: lament the falling-off of wines from the quaintly named Monsieur Clape. St Joseph and Crozes-Hermitage are, depending on your point of view, either the poor relations or the only remotely affordable wines among northern Rhône reds.

The southern Rhône used to be scorned by old-style uptight wine buffs – the wines were simply too loose, warm-hearted and hedonistic for a race brought up in non centrally heated boarding schools on boiled liver and sprouts. Now you should speak of the southern Rhône renaissance and wax lyrical about the eccentric genii of Châteauneuf-du-Pape. These include the wayward Henri Bonneau who makes wonderful wines from a cellar resembling a medieval pigsty and the barmy Jacques Reynaud. Stories abound of the reclusive Reynaud: one authenticated tale concerns a Belgian journalist who turned up for an appointment, waited for twenty minutes, then drove off only to see Reynaud emerging from a drainage ditch.

Another good ploy is to enthuse about white Châteauneuf-du-Pape, specially the Roussanne Vieilles Vignes from Château de Beaucastel. This is so rare that the wine bore is unlikely to have tasted it. With another famous southern Rhône wine, Beaumes-de Venise, the best line is to praise the lesser known red rather than the overexposed sweet white Muscat. The Rhône also produces Tavel, one of the few rosé wines about which it is permissible to be polite.

Vintages: A convenient theory, but unfortunately untrue, is that since the Rhône is so far south vintages don't matter. Another theory also not entirely true is that good vintages in the north are not good in the south and vice versa. 1990, 1994 and 1995 were all good in both; 1991 by contrast was excellent in the north but terrible in the south.

Beaujolais and Mâconnais

These regions are a southern extension of Burgundy and make some attractive red and white wines. It is a pity, therefore, that the wine everybody associates with the region is the generally unpleasant purple beverage, Beaujolais Nouveau. You can make the point that it is hardly surprising Beaujolais Nouveau is unpleasant since it is expressly designed to be:

a) drunk far too young
b) transported from France in various unsuitable ways (fast cars, helicopters, pipelines) for publicity purposes.

Bluffers should only ever proffer a Beaujolais Nouveau which is at least five years old, lightly dismissing anything younger as skilful sales talk.

The Beaujolais to praise are the little-known village wines or **crus**: Fleurie and Moulin-à-Vent, fashionable mainly because they are relatively pronounceable; Brouilly and Côte de Brouilly (which are often just as good) because they are not. Say the newest Cru Regnié does not deserve to be one.

The white Mâcon wines are the nearest non-millionaires can get to white burgundy. The most famous of them, Pouilly-Fuissé (nothing to do with Pouilly-Fumé) is not worth bothering about (unless you are American) because:

a) it is grossly overpriced
b) it is all shipped to America anyway.

Plain Mâcon-Villages is perhaps a little obvious (it can even be found on Chinese restaurant wine lists), but you would do well to mug up some of the individual village names, which are memorably odd, e.g. Mâcon-Lugny (pronounced 'loony') and Mâcon-Prissé. Louis Latour have a good Mâcon-Lugny, Les Genièvres, and Duboeuf have passable Mâcon wines too, such as Mâcon-Villages from the Lenoir estate.

Vintages: Like Burgundy, only less important, is the general rule. 1985 was hailed as the best Beaujolais vintage for 50 years. The same happened with 1988, 1989, 1990 and 1994.

Alsace

Here you must always refer to the wines as 'from Alsace' for, as the great wine writer André Simon once remarked, 'Alsatian is ze dog', and many would agree, especially German wine growers.

The wines of Alsace are an enigma. Part of the problem is confusion of national identity. Alsace-Lorraine has been shunted backwards and forwards between France and Germany so many times that it is no wonder the inhabitants and their wines have become rather schizophrenic. Put simply, they speak French but with a German accent. Or the other way round. For all this confusion Alsace wines used to be remarkably simple and clear. Long before Bulgarian Cabernet Sauvignon and Australian Chardonnay these wines were named after grape varieties (Riesling, Gewürztraminer, Tokay, Pinot Gris, etc.) so that everyone could understand roughly what they were about. This worked so well that the Alsatians decided to complicate matters. They introduced a fiendish hierarchy of grands crus (named vineyards) to run alongside the grape varieties. Now everyone is thoroughly confused but at least the growers can charge higher prices. All rather like Burgundy in fact.

Growers to mention include the impressive and powerfully constructed Zind-Humbrecht (the epithets apply equally to the wines and to Léonard and Olivier Humbrecht), the insanely perfectionist Marcel Deiss and the idiosyncratic André Ostertag. Négociants like Hugel and Trimbach are now considered somewhat old hat – though not as old as the American baseball cap sported by Johnny Hugel.

Germany

German wine has now sunk so low in public esteem that producers have brought in Australian-style labels (Windy Ridge) and English winemaker (Hugh Ryman) in desperate attempts to market it. The culprit in this sorry saga is of course Liebfraumilch (literally, the milk of our dear lady) a technological product hardly known in its land of origin. A possible line of interest here is to praise the 'real' Liebfraumilch – the wine from the tiny Liebfrauen-stiftskirche vineyard next to Worms cathedral. "Unfortunately practically unobtainable" you could add smugly.

Considerable bluffing points may be scored by praising Germany's new wave of Riesling producers – so much more exciting than famous old names such as Deinhard, Schloss Vollrads, Schloss Johannisberg and Bernkasteler Doktor. Enthuse over the quality-minded producers of the Palatinate (or Pfalz if you want to practise those German consonants) such as Rainer Lingenfelder, Pfeffingen, Müller-Catoir and Kurt Darting. Mention the controversial Scheurebe grape which produces wines which smell of cat's pee – "Ah but is it Siamese or Burmese?"

In keeping with their need for order, German wine is governed by the world's most complex and apparently logical grading system. Argue that the whole system is in fact totally illogical (more or less true) and should be scrapped. This saves you the bother of having to learn anything about it.

Italy

Italian wine is like Italian politics. Every now and then a charismatic figure appears, promising to sweep away corruption and abuse and instal a gleaming new system of incredible purity. The wine equivalent of Silvio Berlusconi was Senator Goria, the Minister of Agriculture whose new wine law was introduced with loud fanfares in 1993. The main plank of the law was an exciting new category called IGT, the equivalent of the French vin de pays. Three years later not a single region had applied for IGT and Senator Goria was facing corruption charges.

Well-known names such as Soave, Valpolicella and

Chianti should be greeted with a sour leer, though a few obscure producers such as Pieropan (the Peter Pan of Soave), Quintarelli (Valpolicella) and Riecine (Chianti) may be grudgingly applauded.

Perhaps the most promising group of Italian wines to enthuse about are the so-called Super-Tuscans. Super-Tuscans are not absurdly good-looking people who bomb about the countryside in Maseratis but wines made by absurdly good-looking people who bomb about the countryside in Maseratis. The granddaddy of them all is Sassicaia: demand for this Cabernet Sauvignon-based wine is so intense in Canada that people queue all night for the meagre allocation and then proudly sport a badge saying 'I froze my ass for a bottle of Sass.'

Other names to conjure with include Ornellaia, made by the dashing Marchese Lodovico Antinori, usually seen in the company of gorgeous blondes from St Petersburg; Cepparello, made by Chianti's Paolo de Marchi, and I Sodi Di San Niccolo, now a cult wine in San Francisco.

The other Italian regions with positive bluffing potential are the south, especially Puglia (now crawling with flying winemakers) and the islands of Sardinia and Sicily. All Sicilian wines are absolutely flawless and magnificent, and that comment has nothing to do with a recent visit we received at the Bluffer's Guides from a Signor Montefalco.

Spain and Portugal

Spain has the world's largest acreage of vines but, due to a combination of heat, drought, donkeys, mañana-tendencies and general drift of population towards the costas, does remarkably little with them. There is always Rioja to fall back on and the ubiquitous Catalan firm of Torres – but you should be more ambitious. Claim that Rioja has become predictable – either too oaky or not oaky enough. Praise the handful of single-estate Riojas – Remélluri, Contino, Baron de Ley, Marqués de Murrieta (who used to keep their best 'reservas' in oak for upwards of thirty years until marketing people came along and told them it was unnecessary). Deplore the virtual disappearance of old-fashioned oak-aged white Rioja with the exception of Murrieta (again), CVNE Monopole and Navajas (not the name of a knife-wielding gypsy in a Lorca poem).

The fashionable new areas to bluff in are Ribera (not Ribena as one PR person spelt it) del Duero, Navarra and Rías Baixas (pronounced 'buy-shass'). Say that Ribera's Vega Sicilia is overpriced but rave about Vega Sicilia's new subsidiary cellar Bodegas Alión. The other famous Ribera del Duero wine, Pesquera, has arguably been ruined by its own popularity. Mention the curiously named Ribera del Duero Torremilanos, which, though not expensive, has nothing to do with the budget-priced resort of a similar name.

Navarra used to be considered a poor relation of Rioja but you should argue is now more go-ahead. Praise the sanctioning by the authorities of the French Cabernet Sauvignon grape: recall that in the 19th century Spanish paranoia about French invasions reached such a pitch that the railway gauge was changed at the border.

Rías Baixas, on the Galician coast, is the most fashionable new white wine region. The wine itself, however, should always be called albariño not Rías Baixas.

Praise wines from Lagar de Cervera, Morgadío and Pazo de Barrantes but say the old-styled 'amante' wines from Eulogio Pomares Zénate are even better. Just that name should leave your listener gasping.

Portugal is more problematic, partly because of the stubborn Portuguese adherence to funny old Portuguese grape varieties but also because of pre-historic wine-making technique (leaving wines in old oak or chestnut barrels until they taste of little but acorns). The better-known names in Portuguese table wine Dão (a mixture of dow and dung), Bairrada ('buy-harder'), and Vinho Verde ('vaird') are to be avoided. More bluffing potential is to be found in the previously scorned regions of Alentejo (Borba, Reguengos de Monsaraz) and Ribatejo (Leziria) and Oeste (Arruda).

Eastern Europe

It must be most annoying for the countries of the former Warsaw Pact to continue to be lumped together now they are free and flourishing (well sort of) members of the New Capitalist World Order. Actually alleged political liberalisation has made little or no difference to countries such as Bulgaria and Romania (and we're not just speaking wine): they used to supply cheerful, gluggable reds at bargain prices, and now, after claims by a certain Mr Margrit Todorov that Bulgarian wines would soon be commanding price tags of £100 a bottle, they continue to supply cheerful gluggable reds at bargain prices. Romanian Pinot Noir (which sounds about as probable as Irish caviare) is a wine to mention, and even buy when you're hard up.

Hungary, by contrast, is on the up. Foreign investment has poured in, along with the usual flying winemakers and Chardonnay and Cabernet with Aussie-style labels (Chapel Hill) made by New Zealanders and tasting, well, sort of Chilean. The grand old imperialist dessert wine Tokay has been privatised with French, Spanish and English investment, involving wine's greatest man of letters, Hugh Johnson.

Moldova has sprung to notice, thanks to a partnership linking the Australian firm of Penfolds with a former state farm. Early teething troubles such as most of the grapes being appropriated by peasants at the start of harvest have apparently been sorted out.

Few Russian wines have yet penetrated Western European defences. Some are heavily built and awesomely destructive.

The New World

California

The Californians have approached wine-making with the same manic enthusiasm which they devote to fitness, cuisine and sex. The results have had the same tendency to be larger and glossier than life, but they are now getting better at imitating the subtleties of European wines. Indeed, you should argue that California has gone too far in the direction of so-called 'elegance': Chardonnays, far from the buttery, buxom lovelies of the early 1980s, have tried to imitate anorexic Chablis, and Cabernet Sauvignons have become light and insipid. Yearn for a return to the big blockbuster styles of yesteryear.

Names are a problem in California, because there

are so many of them (the rabbit-like propagation of boutique wineries is becoming a menace) and they are always changing. However, there are a few constant stars. Robert Mondavi continues to be innovative and brilliant: say that his Pinot Noir Reserve is now better even than his Cabernet Sauvignon (and far better than anything from Oregon).

Indeed, proclaim that Californian Pinot Noir is infinitely more exciting than Californian Cabernet and cite Saintsbury, Calera and Au Bon Climat as proof. Or claim that Syrah is now more exciting than Pinot Noir – Qupé and Randall Grahm's whacky Bonny Doon being the key names. Joseph Phelps is reliable. Clos du Val, run by the Frenchman Bernard Portet, is a touchstone for classy Cabernet Sauvignon. In the Napa valley, hillside vineyards are the current concept: Randy Dunn's Cabernet Sauvignon from Howell Mountain and Peter Newton's from Spring Mountain are two of the finest.

It is also possible to impress by the gentle sugges-tion that Napa is overexposed and better value is to be found in the superb Sonoma district – Clos du Bois and Benziger Estate are the names to favour.

Australia

Australians are noted for their pragmatism. About 20 years ago they spotted that all that was needed for wine production was ripe grapes, large-scale industrial manufacturing facilities and simple nomenclature. Some overfastidious souls have complained that Australian wine is all just a bit obvious (or indeed that it all tastes sweet). One such dared to voice this complaint at a Sydney wine show 'The trouble with you, woman,' rasped a voice from the back, 'is that you've never had a wine made from ripe ****ing fruit in yer life.'

Ripeness can be too much of a good thing, even Australians are prepared to admit. In particular the bananas-and-cream-and-brown-sugar style of Australian Chardonnay made with lashings of oak seems to be falling out of favour (though you may robustly state your enjoyment of such unreconstructed examples as Rosemount Show Reserve). A number of influential lean and hungry-looking Australian viticulturalists and oenologists such as Brian Croser, Martin Shaw, Dr Andrew Pirie and Gary Crittenden are preaching the gospel of cool-climate wine-making. This move may seem perverse to most Europeans who struggle to ripen grapes at all in many vintages but it probably makes sense when you're living in a baking dust-bowl.

Cool-climate regions to champion are:

- Margaret River in Western Australia which is not a river, shows no sign of Margaret and is not really cool, but rather on the warm side if truth be told. Wineries to support are Leeuwin for Chardonnay, Cape Mentelle, Cullen (a leading feminist winery) and Moss Wood for everything.
- The Adelaide Hills, home of Brian Croser
- Coonawarra, whose Cabernet Sauvignon can taste like gazpacho.

Cool-climate mania has reached crazy extremes in Tasmania (home of the elegant Dr Pirie) and the bungaloid outskirts of Melbourne, where Garry Crittenden makes Cabernet Sauvignon as unripe as that of Bordeaux in a moderate vintage and just as convincing.

Despite all this, most Australian wine continues to

be made – most effectively – in regions which range from hot (the Barossa – home of Grange Hermitage – Hunter and Clare Valleys) to torrid (the irrigated plains of the Murray River).

Good bluffing gambits – because they are unfairly neglected – are the sweet liqueur muscats, 'stickies' for short, of north-eastern Victoria which after decades of ageing achieve that consistency and taste of black treacle, and the once famed old fortified wines, especially the so-called ports made by Seppelts in the Barossa Valley.

Aussie champagne – whoops, traditional method sparkling wine – is gaining popularity but here you should express a preference for old sparkling Shiraz, preferably on the sweet side. There is simply no answer to this.

New Zealand

When it comes to New Zealand you should dismiss prejudiced notions of a country of colourless crick-eters, Sunday school teachers and sheep. New Zealand wine is more like the modern All Black rugby side – vibrant, fast moving, occasionally aggressive. The runaway success of New Zealand wine has been its remarkably pungent Sauvignon Blanc, often compared to nettles, green gooseberries and ocelot pee.

The best Sauvignon Blancs like the legendary Cloudy Bay (made in the Marlborough region which enjoys exceptionally high sunshine levels) temper the assertiveness of raw Sauvignon with a touch of oak and even a gram or two of residual sugar.

With Cloudy Bay however you should argue that the Chardonnay and even the Cabernet-Merlot are better than the more famous Sauvignon. Other grape

49

varieties you should prefer to Sauvignon are the
unfashionable Riesling (due for a revival as people
have been saying for decades), and the newly fashionable Pinot Noir. Pinot Noir in New Zealand may in
fact be better employed in the production of traditional
method sparkling wine (the stuff we used to call
champagne) which you should praise as potentially
the world's best, not excluding champagne.

South America

Chilean wine is one of the greatest triumphs of modern marketing. The consultants and PR people moved
in the early 1990s to persuade the world that:

a) there had never been any decent Chilean wine
   before
b) everything had changed in Chile after General
   Pinochet stopped being President and became simply Head of the Armed Forces
c) Chile had a vibrant new wine culture.

All these propositions were dodgy at the time although
the last has become truer in the mid-1990s. In fact
Chile has been making excellent Cabernet Sauvignon
since the 1870s, maturing the wine in large vats of the
Chilean wood called raulí. The modernists decreed
that all the raulí should go but you should call for its
reintroduction on the grounds that it at least made
Chilean Cabernet taste different from Bulgarian,
Moldovan, Hungarian, southern French, etc.

Chilean white wine has certainly improved of late,
purportedly because of the discovery of a new cool-
climate vineyard area called the Casablanca Valley
(nothing to do with Bogart and Bergman). Now every
Chilean white wine has the name Casablanca embla-

zoned on it even if the grapes do not come from the Casablanca Valley at all. Don't attempt to explain this confusion. Simply claim that nearly all Chilean white wines seem to be made by the mercurial Ignacio Recabarren.

Be sure to point out two other interesting things about Chile. First, its wine industry goes back to the 1540s. Second, Chile's vineyards have never been affected by phylloxera (see History) because the destructive little vine aphid was, quite simply, unable to cross the Andes.

Other South American wines come from Argentina, which makes an extraordinary quantity of very ordinary wine. Some out-of-the-ordinary wines are the white Torrontés (which tastes, unusually for a wine, of grapes) and the red Malbec, the grape known in France as Cot. Uruguay, Peru and Brazil also make wine: to paraphrase Dr Johnson, it is more the fact that wine is made there than the quality which is of note.

South Africa

South African wine is now on everybody's lips, even better in everyone's mouths, since the establishment of majority rule made it kosher to sell the stuff. Discerning drinkers will avoid cheap blends served up under new ANC-style labels and seek out excellent estate wines such as Klein Constantia, Mulderbosch, Fairview, Kanonkop and Hamilton-Russell. The last has the advantage of impeccable liberal credentials, having opposed apartheid long before the ANC came to power.

WINING AND DINING

It is important to remember that restaurants make most of their profits from wine, and it is not uncommon to find mark-ups of 300-400%. The situation is even worse in France, where greedy restaurateurs push the price of ordinary wine out of the reach of those who need it most. But a mark-up of 100% is considered almost a minimum anywhere and that can hardly be described as generous.

Some restaurants get away with scandalous prices: people fork out double the average high street price for the most basic plonk in unexceptional brasseries without demur. It is depressing to behold. Bear in mind that this wine, often of the most dubious provenance, probably cost the producer the equivalent of a box of matches to make, and even with shipping and duty and a reasonable profit margin for the grower and merchant, can hardly cost the restaurant more than the price of a packet of cigarettes.

When going to a licensed restaurant be aware that you are letting yourself in for an elaborate ritual. Wine waiters are taught to go through various motions, handing the wine list to the most important person, pouring out a little for him or her to taste, but they are rarely taught the purpose of these motions.

For this reason, and because most people are so extraordinarily deferential, wine waiters do not take at all kindly to having their wines sent back. A few simple rules may help you to hold your own:

1. Reject the wine immediately after the waiter has given you a small amount to taste. If you delay, and start drinking, the waiter will understandably assume that:

a) you are unsure of your ground
b) the wine is drinkable.

2. Be polite but firm. Any trace of hesitancy plays right into the hands of the waiter, who invariably assumes the customer is stupid, wrong or trying it on.

3. Only claim to be a wine writer or expert as a last resort and if you are wearing a suit. For some reason waiters do not believe that casually dressed people can know anything about wine.

Of course, this kind of heavy-handed tactic should not be necessary. It can ruin a romantic evening. On the other hand it may also be a good test. A partner who will not allow you to challenge a wine waiter may not be prepared to give you much leeway in other areas.

You should be aware that it is quite rare to be given the right wine in a restaurant in the first place. One vintner, an excessively honest character, sent back a wine which was in fact superior to the one he had ordered only to be told by the waiter that the bottle he had been given in error was 'vairy nice wine, come in fresh today'.

Waiter, This Wine is Corked

It is widely believed that in order to qualify as a real wine expert you need to be able to tell instantly whether or not a wine is corked. In fact no wine term is attended by so much confusion.

Some people, in their innocence, believe that a corked wine has bits of cork floating around in it: this is not the case. Bits of cork, though unsightly, in no way affect the taste of wine. If they did, every bottle would be corked, since the wine inside is constantly in contact with the cork.

Some quite knowledgeable people say that a corked wine tastes of cork. But as not many of us chew cork for fun, it is easier to recognise as wine which smells musty and dank, like a house with rising damp. You might take the line that the word 'corked' is strictly meaningless and that it is much more honest to use the term 'off' – if for no other reason than that it is anathema to the wine expert. But if you want to shine, explain that the problem is caused by "2,4,6 TCA (i.e. Trichloranisole), the chemical compound which is formed in a faulty cork by the action of moulds in the presence of chlorine compounds and phenolics".

There are various kinds of 'off-ness'. Apart from the dank musty odour, there is oxidation. This is what happens when wine is exposed to the atmosphere. It ends up going brown and smelling a bit like toffee. With some wines, especially sherry and madeira, this is actually considered desirable, and the word 'maderised' (i.e. tasting like madeira) is a good term to master and employ when faced with any wine which is tired, old or has been sitting around for far too long. Could be used of some people, come to that.

Additives and Adulterations

Winemakers committing illegal adulteration have been much in the news. First there was anti-freeze (known to bluffers as diethylene glycol), which made wine taste fuller and richer, and did not actually kill anybody, but is poisonous in large doses. So is wine, in really large doses. The bluffer, on that basis, could always try defending anti-freeze.

The second was methanol, which is poisonous in very small doses. It killed quite a number of people, so should probably not be defended.

As a result of these scandals, people started to worry about other substances which are regularly added to wine. These include cultured yeasts (used in Australia), sugar beet, sulphur dioxide, tartaric acid, mud, egg whites, pine resin, dried ox blood and the shredded swim-bladder of the sturgeon. Most of these things are not just harmless but positively beneficial. Point out that people have tried making organic wine, but it tends to taste of manure.

There are a few treatments of wine which can be justifiably condemned. Filtering through asbestos is probably undesirable, and indeed excessive filtering and centrifuging are now considered a bad thing.

If you ever find funny little crystals in the bottom of the glass or bottle, remain calm, smile appreciatively and comment, "Ah, Weinstein – one doesn't see it often enough these days. A sure sign that the wine hasn't been messed about too much." These are tartaric crystals, and are a good thing. Other people may not be convinced, but they should at least be impressed.

Wine and Food

Most wine, of course, cries out to be drunk with food. It is obvious that a fine red burgundy or Californian Cabernet was not made to be drunk on its own. The same is true of the more alcoholic white wines like white burgundy or Sauternes. But some lighter wines, mainly white but occasionally red, are actually more suited for unaccompanied consumption.

The Bach solo violin partitas of the wine world are the great Rieslings of the Mosel-Saar-Ruwer. The Maximin Grünhaus wines of Von Schubert, for instance, are too delicate and fine to have intercourse with any food. The dry Muscats of Alsace are also best drunk as an apéritif. The sweeter German wines, of Auslese standard upwards, are not really pudding wines (they don't have enough alcohol), but wines which form a dessert in themselves. One sip of Trockenbeerenauslese is probably equivalent to a whole slice of Sachertorte. And if you have to have Beaujolais Nouveau, drink it on its own, well chilled.

Funnily enough, some wines which are thought to be best drunk on their own go equally well, if not better, with food. The classic example is sherry. The heavier forms of sherry, amontillado and dry oloroso, are superb with all kinds of soups.

As to the great vexed issue of what wine goes with what food, bluffers should not feel intimidated. The golden rule is that there are *no* golden rules.

The classic axiom is that only white wine can be served with fish. It has to be admitted that most fish dishes are best accompanied by white wines, from Muscadet with shellfish to Meursault with, say, sole in a rich creamy sauce. But the Basque dish of salt cod and ratatouille is so strongly flavoured that it needs a red wine to cope with it, and some dark-fleshed fish like salmon and fresh tuna are particularly well suited to a fairly light red.

You might try some really outrageous combinations (Châteauneuf with oysters, perhaps, or Coquilles St Jacques au Zinfandel) for fun – or at least claim to have tried them.

Burgundy is supposed to be the best wine with game, but you will declare that it all depends on the kind of game. A delicate partridge might be swamped by a heavy Chambertin, for instance, and an equally delicate Margaux might be just the thing. If money is no object, you are supposed to drink Château Yquem ('Ee-kem') with foie gras.

There is also a belief that most cheeses, including the white-rinded ones like brie and camembert, are a particularly suitable accompaniment to the finest Bordeaux (claret). This is not true. White-rinded cheeses completely alter the character of fine red wines, making them taste strangely sweet. Hence the old wine trade adage, 'Sell on cheese, buy on an apple' but this only works with cheaper wines, for Château Lafite with brie is nothing like its true self and might just as well be Beaujolais.

Even cheddar can be too strong and pungent for claret. The only cheeses that go really well with fine red wine are very hard, subtly flavoured ones like the Italian pecorino and the fine Manchego cheeses from Spain. The traditional combination of port and stilton, on the other hand, can be accorded your unqualified respect.

Sherry

Sherry is a fortified wine, like port, except that it is fortified after the fermentation has finished, and so is naturally dry. It is made in a very complicated way, like champagne: you don't need to know how this works, merely its name – the solera system.

People who know about sherry generally go for fino

and manzanilla, the two driest kinds, quite delicious, but only when they are fresh. A half-empty bottle or, worse still, decanter is likely to taste stale and unpleasant. These kinds of sherry should be kept in the fridge and served cold: "Just as they serve it in those tapas bars in Jerez and Sanlúcar de Barrameda". Manzanilla, which comes from the latter town, is always said to have a 'salty tang' as a result of its proximity to the Atlantic ocean. Real amontillado is splendid stuff, but increasingly difficult to find. Like most 'medium' products, it is normally far too sweet. Genuine amontillado is supposed to taste nutty.

Even more bluffing points may be scored by the mention of palo cortado and dry oloroso, now the rarest forms of sherry and excellent with soup.

Port

Port is another of 'the Englishman's wines'. Having lost possession of Bordeaux the British needed another source of wine and Portugal, being rather a sleepy country, was happy to accommodate them. Someone with a sweet tooth then decided that Douro wine tasted nicer if its fermentation was stopped half way through with lots of grape sugar left in. Port has been made that way ever since, and Portugal doesn't seem to have changed much either. There are still a number of English colonials with names like Warre, Graham and Delaforce running around there as if nothing had happened since the 17th century. They have lunch once a week in a place called the Factory House which isn't at all like a factory, and from which

58

foreigners and women are excluded.

The posh kind of port is vintage port. This tastes revolting until it is about 20 years old, and as a result used to be given to boys as a christening present with the idea that it would come of age at the same time as they did. The correct amount to give was a barrel or 'pipe' containing about 50 dozen bottles. Livers must have been stronger in those days: the younger Pitt, in the last week of his final illness, was restricted to one pint of port per day. Nowadays people complain of feeling delicate after a single glass.

Apart from vintage, the only other really good kind of port is old tawny, which is matured in the barrel rather than the bottle. So-called late-bottled vintage port isn't really like vintage port at all – it has no muck in the bottom, for a start. Crusted port, despite not having a vintage, is much more like the real thing (muck included). Ruby port is only suitable for drinking with lemon.

Madeira

Madeira is the only wine to be 'boiled' – deliberately. The process is called the estufa system and involves heating the wine to 120°F (49°C) for a considerable length of time which is what gives it a distinctive burnt flavour. "And all this," you can say knowingly, "is to simulate what happened to madeira when it was used as ballast on sailing ships for the long voyages to Africa and the Indies and accidentally got cooked en route as it crossed and re-crossed the equator."

Madeira is also made from odd grape varieties – Sercial, Verdelho, Bual and Malmsey – or is supposed to be. There is a rumour that these have been supplanted by a much less noble grape called Tinta Negra Mole. Certainly an awful lot of madeira is only fit for sauce. But if you give people a choice between madeira and port they always seem to choose madeira.

Brandy

There are a few simple rules to learn about brandy. The first is that the best brandy is made from the worst wine. The second is that brandy is supposed to get better the longer it stays in the barrel, but does not improve at all once it is in the bottle. Every year a vast amount of brandy in barrels evaporates away: in Cognac they call this the angels' share. If angels can stand young brandy they must have harder heads than humans.

It is important to have an opinion on the question of Cognac versus Armagnac. Cognac is supposed to be more refined and elegant, Armagnac earthier and more robust. It's up to you, but if you are going for Cognac, try to avoid the more commercial brands like Martell, Hennessy and Courvoisier. The connoisseur's brand is Delamain Pale and Dry.

An effective ruse is to have a bottle of very cheap Spanish (Fundador) or Greek (Metaxa 7 Star) brandy in reserve. Bring it out with a flourish, and pour out a huge measure saying, "I have a kind of perverse relish for the really rough stuff – don't you? It hurts like hell, but you can *feel* it doing you good."

GLOSSARY

Appellation – Designated area of wine production protected by elaborate laws which are either ignored or irrelevant.

A.C. – Appellation contrôlée, which applies to French wines from designated regions of which certain standards are demanded. This does not necessarily mean that they are any good.

D.O.C. – Much the same as A.C., only Italian.

Botrytis – A fungus essential to producing really sweet, concentrated wines like Sauternes. Known as 'the noble rot', not to be confused with wine writer's drivel.

Bottle-sick – A temporary condition which affects wines immediately after bottling. Not the condition that affects people after drinking too many bottles.

Cap(sule) – Metal or plastic deterrent which covers the cork. Metal ones are fine, so long as they are made of lead, but there is no known aid for the tough plastic ones.

Cépage – French for grape variety.

Chaptalisation – French for the practice of adding sugar to the must, or unfermented grape juice, named after a chap called Jean Antoine Chaptal who invented it in the 18th century. The French have shrewdly decided that it sounds better than 'the practice of adding sugar'.

Château – a) in France a castle or stately home; b) in Bordeaux, any building, outhouse, shed, in which, or near which, wine is made or stored.

Château-bottled – Wine which is bottled in the aforementioned building, outhouse, shed, etc.

Commune – French for parish.

Cru – French for growth. The best French wines like to call themselves grands crus (great growths), premiers crus (first growths), premiers grands crus, etc.

Extract – That which makes a wine taste nice and isn't alcohol, acidity, fruit or sugar.

Gouleyant – Excellent French word which means gulpable.

Great – Any wine or vintage which is better than average.

Fine – Ethnic term for brandy.

Marc – A kind of brandy made by distilling the skins, pips, etc. Pronounced 'Maaarrh!' Known in Italy as grappa.

Moelleux – French for quite sweet. Difficult word to pronounce even before drinking some.

M.O.G. – American for Matter Other than Grapes, e.g. "I see a little mog has crept in here."

Oechsle – German way of measuring the ripeness of grapes. To talk about Oechsle numbers for wines ('Ah yes, 117 degrees Oechsle – phenomenal') is the equivalent of using Koechel numbers for Mozart's works.

Oenologist – The wine professional's professional, e.g. the controversial Lebanese oenologist Guy Accad who advocates prolonged stewing of the grapes in their skins at low temperature before fermentation. A bit like making jam.

Ordinaire – Undistinguished.

Palate – Soft plate at the back of the mouth which is supposed to be an organ of taste. The palate hasn't got very much to do with taste at all, in fact. People with good palates are supposed to be skilled tasters. A good palate probably just helps you to speak distinctly.

Schistous – Type of flaky slate soil, good for growing vines.

Toffee-nosed – Description of wines which are slightly oxidised. Also applies to some wine writers.

Vin de table/vino da tavola – Wine which will drink you under the table.

THE AUTHOR

Harry Eyres was introduced to serious wine apprecia-
tion – in the form of light Moselle – at the age of
eight. He went on his first tasting trip (to Champagne
and Burgundy) aged 13, and has never looked back
since. With wine running in his blood, in both senses
(his father is a wine merchant), he twice managed to
carry off the coveted individual prize in the Oxford v.
Cambridge Tasting Match (the bibbers' Boat race).

He went on to Christie's Wine Department, and
then spent some time teaching in England and in
Spain, finally deciding to become a full-time writer
for the *Spectator*, the *Times* and various publishers.
Between books, he returns to Spain to anaesthetise
his palate with Fundador brandy in the bars of old
Barcelona.

His main interests seem to be reading, writing and
drinking, not necessarily in that order.